MW01533489

IMAGINATION MOUNTAIN

STORY BY
IVAN MICEK

ILLUSTRATIONS BY
BRENT PLOOSTER
(AND EVERLEY ALVAREZ)

*Buffie family,
Keep playing, imagining + dreaming!
—Ivan*

Hardcover: 979-8-9884946-1-4 • Paperback: 979-8-9884946-2-1 • Kindle: 979-8-9884946-3-8
Library of Congress Control Number and Cataloging in Publication data on file with the Publisher.
Published by Leap Press Books LLC

Production services by Concierge Publishing Services, Omaha, Nebraska
PRINTED IN THE UNITED STATES
10 9 8 7 6 5 4 3 2 1

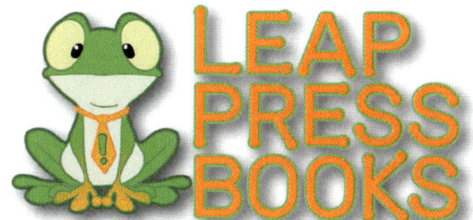

This book is dedicated to Mom,
whose love and nurturing ways created a home
where our imagination was always welcomed, and
to my nieces and nephews for the use of
their likenesses in this book.

Riddle:
What's the most powerful
nation on earth?

Answer:
Imagi-Nation!

LEAP PRESS BOOKS

In my neighborhood, there is a place covered with mountains.

Map by Everley Alvarez

There is one particular mountain
that is bigger and taller than all
the surrounding mountains.
It is so tall that it reaches higher
than the sky.

The mountain is filled with birds, bees, flowers, deer, and every kind of plant and tree that grows on earth, making this mountain a special and magical place.

Everyone who visits this super tall mountain feels like a young child again. They can explore, observe, create, and imagine all day long.

Near the peak of the mountain is a large open area covered with a plush blanket of thick grass. Everyone enjoys playing here.

On one particular day, the sky was sunny and a small group of children played in the open area. After a while, the group became tired.

One by one, they laid down in the grass to rest.

Following a short rest, a boy named Billy sprung up and said, "Let's play a game."

Nikki replied, "I know, I know! Let's take turns finding things that are the colors of the rainbow."

Matt went first. He LQQKed up and shouted,
"I'm LQQKing at the BLUE sky."

Chris, still relaxing on the ground, quickly followed, "I'm resting in the GREEN grass."

Marc said, "LQQK, LQQK, it's an ORANGE ladybug crawling on my hand."

Cassandra, being one who loves flowers, said,
"LQQK at this YELLOW sunflower in my hair."

Just as it was Billy's turn, a cardinal landed on Nikki's shoulder. "LQQK, Billy!"

Billy replied, "Cool! A RED cardinal!"

Nikki said, "That's five colors of the rainbow so far!"

"Now it's my turn to find something purple," Michael said. He LQQKed everywhere, but couldn't even find one purple flower.

Matt said, "There has to be something purple."

Just then, Cassandra had an idea! "Let's put our thinking caps on and use our imaginations to help us find something purple."

The other children agreed and put on their thinking caps to think of something purple.

Suddenly, Chris jumped up and LQQKed through the super-duper mountain-view imagiscope, "I see something purple. The trees are PURPLE!"

The other children began laughing and Michael said, "They are not purple. LQQK, they are GREEN!"

Chris replied, "When I use my imagination, the trees are PURPLE."

Soon Marc exclaimed, "I can see PURPLE trees, too!"

It wasn't long before all the children agreed that in fact the trees were PURPLE! By using their imaginations, the trees could be any color they imagined them to be.

The mountain proved that the children can imagine anything to be exactly what they want.

Billy exclaimed, "The stars are RED!"

Matt said, "The moon is GREEN!"

Cassandra chimed in, "Yes! And the sun is BLUE!"

Michael shouted, "And, yes! The trees are PURPLE!"

Marc said, "I have an idea. Let's call it IMAGINATION MOUNTAIN!"

The children returned to their homes, knowing this mountain was Imagination Mountain, a place that is wherever they want it to be. It's a special and magical place where they can play, imagine and dream.

What does YOUR Imagination Mountain LQQK like? Write a poem, draw a picture, start a short story, invent a machine, save the world. Use this space to let your imagination imagine!

Artist's First Name:_____ Date: _____